Alif Baa

Al-Kitaab Arabic Language Program

دليل الإجابات

Answer Key for
Alif Baa

مدخل الى حروف العربية وأصواتها

Introduction to Arabic Letters and Sounds

Third Edition • الطبعة الثالثة

كرستن بروستاد Kristen Brustad
محمود البطل Mahmoud Al-Batal
عباس التونسي Abbas Al-Tonsi

∞ This book is printed on acid-free paper meeting the requirements of the American National Standard for Permanence in Paper for Printed Library Materials.

15 14 13 12 11 10   9 8 7 6 5 4 3 2

Printed in the United States of America

Unit One الوحدة الأولى

Drill 1. Differentiating the *th* sounds

Answers: <u>three:</u> thumb, teeth, throb, think, through, thought, theft, depth

  <u>that:</u> they, there, thus, although, brother, together, weather, bother, then, rather

Unit Two الوحدة الثانية

Drill 1. Hearing frontal and deep alif

1. D	2. F	3. D	4. D	5. F	6. F
7. D	8. F	9. F	10. D	11. F	12. D

Drill 2. Dictation

6. بات	5. باب	4. تابا	3. باتا	2. تاب	1. با

Drill 3. Word recognition

6. ثبت	5. ثابت	4. بث	3. ثاب	2. بتات	1. بات

Drill 4. Dictation

4. تابوت	3. توب	2. توت	1. ثاب

Drill 5. Dictation

1. ثوبا   2. بيتي   3. بيتا   4. باتي

Drill 6. Distinguishing between long and short vowels

1. b   2. a   3. a   4. b   5. a   6. b

Drill 7. Identifying long and short vowels

1. L   2. S   3. L   4. S   5. L   6. S

7. S   8. S   9. L   10. L   11. S   12. L

Drill 8. FatHa dictation

1. تَثبيت   2. بَتات   3. باتَت   4. ثَبات   5. ثَبَت   6. ثابَت

Drill 10. Short vowel dictation

1. ثَبُتَت   2. ثُبتُ   3. تَبيت   4. تَتوب   5. تَثبُت   6. ثُبوت

Drill 11. Dictation

1. بابي   2. توبي   3. ثُبوت   4. توبا

5. تَبيت   6. ثَبات   7. تابَت   8. ثوبي

Drill 13. Letter connection

| 1. باتا | 2. ثَباتي | 3. بابا | 4. ثَبَتَ | 5. بابي | 6. توبي |
| 7. تُبَتَ | 8. توبا | 9. تُثِبِتي | 10. تَبيت | 11. بيبي | |

Unit Three الوحدة الثالثة

Drill 1. Dictation

| 1. جاب | 2. تاج | 3. جوبي | 4. جُبَب | 5. جُثَث | 6. جيب |

Drill 2. Dictation

| 1. حوت | 2. بَحث | 3. حَبيب | 4. تَحت | 5. بوحي | 6. باحَت |

Drill 3. Recognizing ج, ح, and خ

| 1. خ | 2. ج | 3. ح | 4. خ | 5. ح | 6. ح |
| 7. خ | 8. ح | 9. ج | 10. ج | 11. خ | 12. ج |

Drill 4. Letter connection

| 1. خابَت | 2. حِجاب | 3. حَبيب | 4. تُخوت |
| 5. تَجوب | 6. بُحوث | 7. تَبوحي | 8. حَجَبَت |

Drill 5. Dictation

| 1. حَجَبَ | 2. باخ | 3. تَختي | 4. حاج | 5. باحِث | 6. جابَت |

Drill 7. Dictation

4. ثَواب   3. جَواب   2. تَبْويب   1. خَوْخ

Drill 8. Dictation

4. يَحْجُب   3. جُيوبي   2. حَياتي   1. ثِياب

Drill 10. Letter connection

5. جيبوتي   4. ثِيابي   3. خَوْخ   2. حُجُب   1. جابَت

10. جُيوب   9. بُيوت   8. واجِبات   7. بُحوث   6. حَبيبتي

Drill 11. Dictation

6. تَحْتاج   5. يَحْجُب   4. يَخيب   3. يَبوح   2. بَيْتي   1. واجِب

Unit Four   الوحدة الرابعة

Drill 1. Recognizing hamza

1. Yes	2. No	3. Yes	4. No	5. Yes	6. No
7. Yes	8. No	9. Yes	10. No	11. Yes	12. Yes

Drill 2. Dictation

6. أَتَت   5. باء   4. أَخي   3. أثاث   2. أَب   1. ثاء

Drill 3. Distinguishing initial hamza, و, and ي

1. أُ   2. و   3. إ   4. ي   5. و   6. إ

Drill 7. Distinguishing between ث and ذ

1. ث   2. ذ   3. ذ   4. ذ   5. ث   6. ذ

7. ث   8. ث   9. ذ   10. ذ   11. ذ   12. ث

Drill 8. Reviewing the difference between ث and ذ

٤. ث   ٣. ذ   ٢. ذ   ١. ذ

٨. ذ   ٧. ث   ٦. ذ   ٥. ث

Drill 9. Letter connection

٤. حُروب   ٣. زَرَد   ٢. خادِر   ١. رَذاذ

٨. حُدود   ٧. أزْواج   ٦. بِحار   ٥. رَجاء

١٢. يَخْرُج   ١١. أدْوار   ١٠. تَحْذير   ٩. رُدود

١٤. ذَبَحَت   ١٣. تَجارِب

Drill 10. Dictation

٥. ذُباب   ٤. زَوْجات   ٣. واحِد   ٢. أبي   ١. أُخْت

١٠. أحْزاب   ٩. يُريد   ٨. رَباب   ٧. أزْرار   ٦. دَجاج

Drill 13. Dialing the telephone

1. 01-355-6791	2. 05-923-761	3. 703-856-9421	4. 70-724-3695
5. 678-924-3090	6. 416-290-0874	7. 044-694-8015	8. 010-768-1705
9. 944-304-667	10. 20-2-766-9143		

Unit Five   الوحدة الخامسة

Drill 1. Identifying shadda

1. Yes	2. Yes	3. No	4. No	5. Yes	6. Yes
7. No	8. Yes	9. No	10. Yes	11. No	12. Yes

Drill 2. Identifying shadda and long vowels

٦. ا   ٥. ي   ٤. ـّ   ٣. ـّ   ٢. ا   ١. ـّ

١٢. ا   ١١. ـّ   ١٠. ـّ   ٩. ي   ٨. ـّ   ٧. و

Drill 3. Dictation

٦. تَجَرَّد   ٥. دَرَّب   ٤. جَرَّب   ٣. بَوّاب   ٢. زَوَّر   ١. خَبّاز

Drill 4. Dictation

٦. تَحْسُب   ٥. وَسْواس   ٤. يَتَجَسَّس   ٣. سَرْدي   ٢. سادِس   ١. سَراب

Drill 5. Dictation

٦. تَرْشيح   ٥. شَجَر   ٤. حَشيش   ٣. أَشْدو   ٢. تَشْديد   ١. يُبَشِّر

Drill 7. Distinguishing between س and ص

1. س	2. ص	3. ص	4. س	5. ص	6. س
7. س	8. ص	9. ص	10. ص	11. س	12. ص

Drill 8. Identifying ص and س

٥. س	٤. ص	٣. س	٢. ص	١. س
		٨. ص	٧. ص	٦. ص

Drill 10. Dictation

٦. يَصْرُخ   ٥. صَبْري   ٤. صَوَّر   ٣. صَباح   ٢. باص   ١. صابِر

Drill 11. Contrasting د and ض

٦. د	٥. د	٤. ض	٣. ض	٢. ض	١. د
١٢. ض	١١. د	١٠. ض	٩. ض	٨. د	٧. ض

Drill 12. Recognizing د and ض

٥. د	٤. ض	٣. د	٢. ض	١. ض
	٩. ض	٨. ض	٧. د	٦. د

Drill 14. Letter connection

٥. اِسْتيراد   ٤. تَصْدير   ٣. أسْرار   ٢. شَبابي   ١. صَبور

١٠. صَباح   ٩. إشارات   ٨. شَوارِب   ٧. خَضْرَوات   ٦. صَواريخ

١٤. تَخَصُّصات   ١٣. تَرَضْرَضَت   ١٢. صَراصير   ١١. صُوَري

Drill 15. Dictation

٥. ضَباب   ٤. سَوْداء   ٣. رِياض   ٢. صَيّاد   ١. سَيِّد

١٠. ضَريح   ٩. حاضِر   ٨. ضَجَر   ٧. صَحيح   ٦. صارِخ

Unit Six   الوحدة السادسة

Drill 1. Listening for ة

1. Yes	2. No	3. Yes	4. No	5. Yes	6. Yes
7. No	8. No	9. Yes			

Drill 2. Recognizing ط

1. b	2. a	3. b	4. a	5. a
6. a	7. b	8. b	9. b	10. a

Drill 3. Identifying ط

1. No	2. Yes	3. No	4. Yes	5. Yes	6. Yes
7. Yes	8. No	9. No	10. Yes		

Drill 4. Identifying ت and ط

1. ط	2. ط	3. ت	4. ط	5. ط
6. ط	7. ت	8. ت	9. ت	

Drill 6. Dictation

٦. شُرْطي   ٥. طَيِّب   ٤. طُيور   ٣. حَطَب   ٢. طازَج   ١. طار

Drill 7. Recognizing ظ

1. b	2. a	3. b	4. a	5. b
6. a	7. b	8. b	9. b	10. a

Drill 8. Distinguishing ث , ذ , ض , and ظ

1. ظ	2. ث	3. ظ	4. ذ	5. ض
6. ظ	7. ذ	8. ض	9. ث	10. ذ

Drill 10. Identifying ث , ذ , and ظ

٥. ث	٤. ث	٣. ظ	٢. ذ	١. ظ
١٠. ذ	٩. ذ	٨. ث	٧. ذ	٦. ث

Drill 11. Dictation

٤. ظَبي	٣. بوظة	٢. يَحُثّ	١. حَظْر
٨. حَظّي	٧. ثُبوت	٦. حوذي	٥. حَذَر

Drill 14. Identifying ء and ع

1. ع	2. ء	3. ع	4. ء	5. ع
6. ء	7. ع	8. ع	9. ء	

Drill 16. Distinguishing between ء and ع

٥. ع	٤. ء	٣. ع	٢. ع	١. ع
٩. ع	٨. ء	٧. ع	٦. ع	

Drill 17. Dictation

٤. رَبيع	٣. بَعيد	٢. عَروس	١. يَعيش
٨. عَجيب	٧. أَسْعار	٦. جاعَت	٥. سَعودي

Drill 18. Distinguishing between غ and خ

1. خ	2. غ	3. خ	4. غ	5. غ
6. خ	7. خ	8. غ	9. خ	

Drill 20. Identifying غ and خ

٥. خ	٤. غ	٣. غ	٢. غ	١. غ
	٩. غ	٨. خ	٧. خ	٦. غ

Drill 21. Letter connection

٤. شَخْصِيّة	٣. بَعيد	٢. تَغَيُّرات	١. صَراحة
٨. أَطِبّاء	٧. غَرْبِيّة	٦. طُرودي	٥. اِسْتَغْرَب
	١١. تَصْغير	١٠. ضَواحي	٩. شَظايا
		١٣. رُسْغ	١٢. تَخَصُّص

Drill 22. Word recognition

5. صَرير	4. صاع	3. إصبـع	2. دَرَز	1. غَرب
	9 عَبَّر	8. صَبي	7. حَظَر	6. حُثّ

Drill 23. Dictation

٥. بَغَت	٤. صَغير	٣. يُغَيِّر	٢. خاسِر	١. طاغي
١٠. صَبّاغ	٩. أَسْعار	٨. غَرْبي	٧. شارِع	٦. بَعيد

Unit Seven الوحدة السابعة

Drill 1. Dictation

٥. عَفاف   ٤. وَفاء   ٣. صَفاء   ٢. فَوْزِيّة   ١. فَرَح

١٠. فَتْحي   ٩. عَفيف   ٨. فَريد   ٧. فَوْزي   ٦. فايِز

Drill 2. Hearing ق

1. No   2. Yes   3. Yes   4. No   5. Yes

6. Yes   7. Yes   8. No   9. No

Drill 3. Dictation

٦. طابِق   ٥. بَرْقوق   ٤. زُقاق   ٣. حُقوق   ٢. إِبْريق   ١. أَقارِب

Drill 4. Distinguishing between ق and ك

1. ك   2. ق   3. ق   4. ك   5. ق   6. ق

7. ك   8. ق   9. ق   10. ك   11. ق   12. ق

Drill 6. Identifying ق and ك

٥. ق   ٤. ق   ٣. ق   ٢. ق   ١. ق

٩. ك   ٨. ك   ٧. ك   ٦. ق

Drill 7. Dictation

٦. تَحكي ٥. كاكاو ٤. ذاكِرة ٣. عَساكِر ٢. كِفاح ١. أفْكار

Drill 8. Dictation

٥. ألعاب ٤. حَلال ٣. ذُيول ٢. قَليل ١. حَليب

١٠. بِلاد ٩. لاعِب ٨. كِلابي ٧. أخْوال ٦. بَصَل

Drill 9. Word recognition

٥. صَقَل ٤. فِقرة ٣. عِقال ٢. أطَلّ ١. قَلْب

١٠. بَلَع ٩. خُذي ٨. تَقدير ٧. ظَرف ٦. رَكَض

Drill 10. Sound recognition

٥. ع ٤. ط ٣. ض ٢. غ ١. ع

١٠. ص ٩. ص ٨. غ ٧. ط ٦. ض

١٤. ض ١٣. ذ ١٢. ض ١١. ظ

Drill 11. Dictation

٣. جَواب صَحيح ٢. سَندويش فَلافِل ١. وَرَقة بَيْضاء

٦. قِطّة سَوْداء ٥. فكرة غَريبة ٤. شَباب عَرَب

Unit Eight الوحدة الثامنة

Drill 1. Dictation

١. مَحْمود   ٢. زَميل   ٣. مَعْمول   ٤. كَلام

٥. مَدارِس   ٦. ظالِم   ٧. مَلاليم   ٨. مُشْمِس

Drill 2. Dictation

١. لُبْنان   ٢. حَنان   ٣. قَوانين   ٤. نَعْرِف   ٥. مَمْنون

٦. نِظام   ٧. بِنايات   ٨. جَوانِب   ٩. نُجوم   ١٠. مُغَنّي

Drill 3. Distinguishing between ـه and ح

1. ـه   2. ـه   3. ح   4. ـه   5. ح   6. ح

7. ـه   8. ح   9. ـه   10. ـه   11. ح   12. ـه

Drill 5. Distinguishing between ـه and ح

١. ـه   ٢. ـه   ٣. ـه   ٤. ح   ٥. ح   ٦. ـه

٧. ح   ٨. ح   ٩. ـه   ١٠. ح   ١١. ـه   ١٢. ح

Drill 6. Dictation

١. كاهِن   ٢. فَهْم   ٣. هَناء   ٤. فُلوسُهُم   ٥. هَياكِل   ٦. ضاهِر

Drill 8. Word recognition

٦. عائب	٥. عرق	٤. صورة	٣. غلاب	٢. قرع	١. زأر
١٢. قبس	١١. صر	١٠. ثائر	٩. قباب	٨. سعل	٧. تفاعل

Drill 9. Letter connection

٥. غَرائِب	٤. أكلات	٣. وَظيفَة	٢. ظُروفي	١. تَساؤُل
١٠. ضَرورات	٩. خَليفَة	٨. إفريقْيا	٧. فَوائِد	٦. جَحافِل
١٥. طَماطِم	١٤. مَذاهِب	١٣. كَريم	١٢. أنْهار	١١. أظافِري
٢٠. تَعْظيم	١٩. كَهْرَباء	١٨. آكُلُها	١٧. كَلامُه	١٦. نِهايات
			٢٢. أسْئِلَة	٢١. غُفْران

Unit Nine الوحدة التاسعة

Drill 1. Reading الـ aloud

٤. الطّائِرة	٣. المَدينة	٢. البَيت	١. الدّكتور
٨. الدّيـمُقراطي	٧. الصّفّ	٦. الكَعبة	٥. الشّارع
١٢. العَيْن	١١. اللَّوح	١٠. السَّيارة	٩. القُرآن
١٦. الظّلام	١٥. النَّهر	١٤. السّؤال	١٣. الغَزال
٢٠. الثَّقافة	١٩. الخَير	١٨. الحِزب	١٧. الإسلام

Drill 2. Recognizing الـ

1. Yes	2. Yes	3. No	4. No	5. Yes	6. No
7. Yes	8. Yes	9. No	10. Yes	11. Yes	12. Yes

Drill 3. Word recognition

٥. أقلام   ٤. النهاية   ٣. أعمل   ٢. الصفّ   ١. السلام

١٠. أنـور   ٩. الثاني   ٨. الظلام   ٧. الصباح   ٦. أصوم

Drill 4. Listening for الـ and word boundaries in phrases

1. Yes   2. Yes   3. No   4. Yes

5. No   6. Yes   7. Yes   8. Yes

Drill 6. Dictation

٥. الصّباح   ٤. أَفْعال   ٣. السَّماء   ٢. الأَنهار   ١. الطُّلّاب

١٠. الْخَير   ٩. الصّغير   ٨. السَّلام   ٧. السّيّارة   ٦. الْغُرفة

١٢. أَدْوار   ١١. الشّاي

Drill 7. Identifying همزة and وصلة

٤. لي أَسْنان   ٣. عِندي أَلم   ٢. مع الشّاي   ١. والِدي أُستاذ

٧. هُوَ أَحمد   ٦. أين ٱلبيت؟   ٥. صديقي ٱلفرنسي

١٠. أنا ٱلأستاذ   ٩. أخو ٱلبنت   ٨. في ٱلمدينة

Drill 9. Names of Arab countries

٣. الجَزائِر الجَزائِر   ٢. موريتانيا نَواكشوط   ١. الْمَغرِب الرِّباط

٦. مِصر القاهِرة   ٥. ليبيا طَرابُلُس   ٤. تونِس تونِس

٧. السّودان الخَرطوم ٨. الصّومال موقَديشو/مُقَديشو ٩. الأُردُن عَمّان

١٠. إسرائيل وفِلَسطين القُدس ١١. لُبنان بَيْروت ١٢. سوريا دِمَشق

١٣. العِراق بَغداد ١٤. الكُوَيْت الكُوَيْت ١٥. السَّعوديّة الرِّياض

١٦. قَطَر الدَّوحة ١٧. البَحرَيْن المَنامة ١٨. الإمارات أَبو ظَبي

١٩. عُمان مَسقَط ٢٠. اليَمَن صَنعاء

Drill 16. Using the Arabic-English glossary

١. مبسوط ٢. مرحبا ٣. تفضل ٤. طالب ٥. طاولة

٦. مكتب ٧. امتحان ٨. تمرين ٩. ممكن ١٠. واسع

COMPONENTS OF THE AL-KITAAB LANGUAGE PROGRAM

Alif Baa: Introduction to Arabic Letters and Sounds
Third Edition

Student Book
ISBN 978-1-58901-632-3, paperback with DVD bound in
ISBN 978-1-58901-644-6, hardcover with DVD bound in
(Only audio and video materials on DVD)

Teacher's Edition
ISBN 978-1-58901-705-4, paperback with DVD and answer key bound in

Answer Key to Alif Baa (only needed if not using companion website)
ISBN 978-1-58901-634-7, paperback

DVD for Alif Baa
ISBN 978-1-58901-633-0, DVD-ROM

Companion Website available at alkitaabtextbook.com
....

Part One
Al-Kitaab fii Ta^callum al-^cArabiyya with DVDs: A Textbook for Beginning Arabic,
Part One
Second Edition
ISBN 978-1-58901-104-5, paperback with 3 DVDs bound in
(All multimedia combined on DVD)

Answer Key to Al-Kitaab, Part One with DVDs
Second Edition
ISBN 978-1-58901-037-6, paperback

THIRD EDITION COMING IN SPRING 2011
....

Part Two
Al-Kitaab fii Ta^callum al-^cArabiyya with DVDs: A Textbook for Arabic, Part Two
Second Edition
ISBN 978-1-58901-096-3, paperback with 3 DVDs bound in
(All multimedia combined on DVD)

Answer Key to Al-Kitaab, Part Two with DVDs
Second Edition
ISBN 978-1-58901-097-0, paperback

....

Part Three
Al-Kitaab fii Ta^callum al-^cArabiyya with DVD and MP3 CD: A Textbook for Arabic, Part Three
ISBN 978-1-58901-149-6, paperback with DVD and MP3 CD bound in

....

Audio On the Go
These CDs contain MP3 files of the audio only from the *Al-Kitaab, Second Edition* volumes. Perfect for those students who want the portability of MP3 files for practice, these files can be transferred to an MP3 device, played on a computer, or played on some home CD players.

Al-Kitaab Part One Audio On the Go ISBN 978-1-58901-150-2
Al-Kitaab Part Two Audio On the Go ISBN 978-1-58901-151-9

For price and ordering information, visit our website at www.press.georgetown.edu or call 800-537-5487.
For more information on teaching the *Al-Kitaab* language program, visit www.alkitaabtextbook.net.

**GEORGETOWN
UNIVERSITY PRESS
LANGUAGES**